THE CAPITOL

Lyn Sirota

www.av2books.com

AV² provides enriched content that supplements and complements this book. Weigl's AV² books strive to create inspired learning and engage young minds in a total learning experience.

Your AV² Media Enhanced books come alive with...

 Audio
Listen to sections of the book read aloud.

 Key Words
Study vocabulary, and complete a matching word activity.

 Video
Watch informative video clips.

 Quizzes
Test your knowledge.

 Embedded Weblinks
Gain additional information for research.

 Slide Show
View images and captions, and prepare a presentation.

 Try This!
Complete activities and hands-on experiments.

... and much, much more!

Go to **www.av2books.com**, and enter this book's unique code.

BOOK CODE

T 5 9 1 0 0

AV² by Weigl brings you media enhanced books that support active learning.

Published by AV² by Weigl
350 5th Avenue, 59th Floor
New York, NY 10118

Website: www.av2books.com   www.weigl.com

Library of Congress Cataloging-in-Publication Data
Sirota, Lyn A., 1963-
The Capitol / Lyn Sirota.
    pages cm. -- (Virtual field trip)
Includes index.
  ISBN 978-1-62127-460-5 (hardcover : alk. paper) -- ISBN 978-1-62127-466-7 (softcover : alk. paper)
1. United States Capitol (Washington, D.C.)--Juvenile literature. 2. Washington (D.C.)--Buildings, structures, etc. I. Title.
F204.C2S57 2013
975.3--dc23
                        2012041044

Printed in the United States of America in North Mankato, Minnesota
1 2 3 4 5 6 7 8 9 0 17 16 15 14 13

032013
WEP301112

Editor: Heather Kissock
Design: Terry Paulhus

Every reasonable effort has been made to trace ownership and to obtain permission to reprint copyright material. The publishers would be pleased to have any errors or omissions brought to their attention so that they may be corrected in subsequent printings.

Weigl acknowledges Getty Images as its primary image supplier for this title.

10 15

Contents

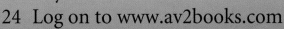

What Is the Capitol?

The Capitol sits majestically at the end of the National **Mall** in Washington, District of Columbia (D.C.). Its dome rises high above the surrounding buildings. Those who encounter the Capitol immediately recognize it as the **focal point** of the United States **legislature**. It is a national landmark and one of the most historic and recognizable structures in the world.

For more than two centuries, the Capitol has been the place where members of Congress debate and pass the nation's laws. The United States has a **bicameral** government. The two government bodies that make up Congress, the Senate and the House of Representatives, are both housed within the Capitol's walls.

Prior to the construction of the Capitol, Congress did not have a permanent home. In the country's early years, Congress met in Philadelphia, Pennsylvania. It later moved to New Jersey and Maryland before settling for a short time in New York. By 1790, the government realized that it needed to have a national capital. It decided to create a city called Washington to fill this role. As the capital city for the entire country, Washington needed a building to house the federal government. This building was to be called the Capitol.

The Capitol stands as a monument to America's citizens and their government.

Snapshot of the District of Columbia

The District of Columbia is located in the northeast United States. It covers an area of 69 square miles (179 square kilometers) and sits on the Virginia-Maryland border. The district is separated from Virginia by the Potomac River.

INTRODUCING D.C.

CAPITAL CITY: Washington

FLAG:

MOTTO: *Justia Omnibus* (Justice for All)

NICKNAME: The Nation's Capital

POPULATION: 617,996 (2011)

FOUNDED: July 16, 1790

CLIMATE: Subtropical, with four distinct seasons

SUMMER TEMPERATURE: Average of 79° Fahrenheit (26° Celsius)

WINTER TEMPERATURE: Average of 38°F (3°C)

TIME ZONE: Eastern Standard Time (EST)

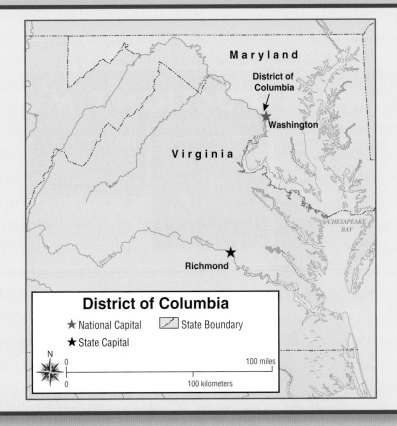

Maryland

District of Columbia

Washington

Virginia

CHESAPEAKE BAY

Richmond

District of Columbia

★ National Capital   State Boundary
★ State Capital

N

0   100 miles
0   100 kilometers

District of Columbia Symbols

The District of Columbia has several official symbols. Some symbols represent the features that distinguish the area from other parts of the United States. Others indicate the unique place D.C. has in the history of the country.

OFFICIAL FLOWER
American Beauty Rose

OFFICIAL BIRD
Wood Thrush

OFFICIAL TREE
Scarlet Oak

A Step Back in Time

Once the decision was made to create the nation's capital city, the government began searching for people to plan the city's layout. A French **engineer** named Pierre Charles L'Enfant submitted his idea for a 1-mile (1.6-km) long roadway that would link the city's "Congress House," or Capitol, with the president's official residence. A contest was then held to find the best design for the Capitol. The winning entry came from Dr. William Thornton, a Scottish-trained physician.

CONSTRUCTION TIMELINE

1793 AD
President George Washington lays the Capitol's **cornerstone** on September 18, and construction begins.

1800
The Senate **Wing** is completed, and Congress holds its first session in the building.

1811
The House Wing is completed.

1814
The building is damaged when British soldiers set fire to it during the **War of 1812**. Plans are made to restore the building to its original condition.

1819
The Capitol **restoration** project is completed. As part of the restoration, the dome is enlarged.

George Washington was the U.S. president from 1789 to 1797.

The burning of Washington took place on August 24, 1814. British soldiers set fire to both the Capitol and the White House, along with several other important public buildings.

Thornton's design went through several changes before construction began. Several **architects**, including Stephen Hallet and James Hoban, were brought in to rework the design and supervise the building's construction. Construction finally began in 1793.

Over the years, the Capitol has had 11 architects. Some were involved in the building's original construction. Others planned extensions and renovations.

1850

Work begins on the construction of two new wings that are needed to accommodate the growing number of government workers.

1855

The existing wooden dome is removed. Construction begins on a new, fireproof, **cast iron** dome.

1962

The East front extension, which adds another 90 rooms to the building, is completed. A subway terminal is constructed under the Senate steps.

2008

The U.S. Capitol Visitor Center opens. Located underground on the east side of the Capitol, it contains exhibits, theaters, and displays.

It took more than 10 years to construct the Capitol dome. Construction was completed in 1866.

The visitor center covers nearly 580,000 square feet (53,884 square meters), almost three quarters the size of the Capitol itself.

The Capitol's Location

The Capitol was built on a piece of land called Jenkins Hill. This is a raised area at the east end of the National Mall, the long roadway that joins the Capitol to the White House. The site was chosen for its elevation. The city planners wanted the Capitol to be located in a place where its importance could be showcased. Today, Jenkins Hill is called Capitol Hill.

Washington, D.C., was built around the Capitol. The city is divided into four **quadrants** called the Northwest, the Southwest, the Northeast, and the Southeast. The U.S. Capitol building is where these four quadrants meet.

The Capitol is located in the middle of a 58-acre (23.5-hectare) park. The entire grounds surrounding the Capitol cover about 274 acres (111 ha).

The Capitol Today

Today, the Capitol remains the center of the United States legislature. Decisions regarding the country and its citizens are made here on a daily basis. Many of these decisions affect people in other countries as well. As a result, the building has become a major international tourist attraction. It is estimated that approximately three million visitors tour the Capitol every year.

Area The Capitol covers a ground area of 175,170 square feet (16,274 square meters). The total floor area is 1.5 million square feet (139,355 sq. m).

Height From the building's base to the top of the dome, the Capitol stands 289 feet (88 m) tall. The dome itself is 217 feet (66 m) tall.

289 feet (88 m)

Length and Width The Capitol is 751 feet (229 m) long. Its widest point measures 350 feet (107 m).

Outside the Capitol

*The Capitol is an example of 19th-century neoclassical architecture. This style is known for its use of symmetry, tall columns, domed roofs, and **pediments**.*

Symmetry The Capitol was designed so that each side is in balance with the other. This means that both the left and right sides of the building share the same features in exactly the same place. Windows, columns, and doorways are placed in the exact position on each side of the building. As a result of this placement, the center of the building becomes the focal point.

Neoclassical buildings are based on the architecture of ancient Greece and Rome. Symmetry is a major feature of this style of building.

Corinthian columns are found on the Capitol's East Front.

Columns Columns are one of the Capitol's key features. They serve as a decorative element inside and outside the building. The exterior of the Capitol has both Corinthian and Ionic columns. Corinthian columns have elaborate sculptures at the top. Ionic columns are capped with large **scrolls**.

Porticoes The Capitol has four porticoes, or columned porches. The North Portico serves as the entrance to the Senate, while the South Portico leads to the House of Representatives. The West Portico faces the back of the building. The East Portico is the main entrance to the Capitol. Framed by 24 marble columns, this portico features several sculptures that represent the history and **ideals** of the country.

Many U. S. presidents take the oath of office on the East Portico.

Statue The *Statue of Freedom* is the crowning feature of the Capitol's dome. Made of bronze, it stands 19.5 feet (6 m) tall and weighs approximately 15,000 pounds (6,800 kilograms). The statue shows Freedom wearing a flowing gown. Her right hand rests on a sword, while her left hand holds a wreath of victory and the shield of the United States. Her helmet is encircled by stars and has an eagle's head, feathers, and talons.

The items on Freedom's helmet honor the country's American Indians.

Pediments

Three of the four porticoes are capped by a pediment. Each of these pediments features a symbolic sculpture. The sculpture over the East Portico is called *Genius of America*. It features the figures of America, Justice, Hope, and an eagle. The sculpture on the Senate pediment is called *Progress of Civilization*. It shows America surrounded by its citizens. The House pediment has a sculpture called *Apotheosis of Democracy*. It shows Peace protecting Genius.

The Genius of America pediment is 81.5 feet (24.8 m) long. The figures of America, Justice, and Hope are 9 feet (2.7 m) tall.

Congress budgeted $100,000 to construct the dome in 1855. By the time it was finished, more than $1 million had been spent.

Dome The Capitol's dome is actually made up of two separate domes. The interior dome sits inside the more visible exterior dome. The dome is made from 8,909,200 pounds (4,041,145 kg) of cast iron. Forty-eight columns encircle the exterior dome. **Pilasters** and windows provide other forms of decoration.

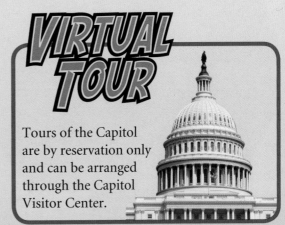

VIRTUAL TOUR

Tours of the Capitol are by reservation only and can be arranged through the Capitol Visitor Center.

Inside the Capitol

The interior of the Capitol continues the neoclassical design of the exterior. The building contains several areas that have symbolic meaning to U.S. citizens.

The Rotunda includes the interior of the Capitol's dome. It rises 180 feet (55 m) above the Rotunda's floor.

Rotunda The Rotunda is an impressive domed, circular room in the center of the Capitol. It is located on the second floor. The dome's ceiling features a painting called *The Apotheosis of Washington*. It pays tribute to George Washington and his contributions to the country. Other paintings of historic events decorate the Rotunda walls. Separating the dome and the walls is a **frieze** that shows important events from U.S. history.

The columns in the Crypt are made from brown stone and are connected by sandstone arches.

Crypt The Crypt is a large circular area on the first floor. It is located directly under the Rotunda. The room has 40 columns that support the floor of the Rotunda. The center of the Crypt's floor features a large star pattern. The star signifies the point from which all of the city's streets were planned and numbered. Thirteen statues have been placed around the Crypt. These statues represent the country's original 13 colonies.

The House Chamber has no windows. It was constructed this way so that the people inside would not be distracted by outside noise.

House Chamber The House Chamber is also known as the Hall of the House of Representatives. It is a large meeting room in the center of the Capitol's south wing. Members of the House of Representatives sit in a semicircle on platforms that face the Speaker's desk at the front of the room. The Speaker controls the discussions that take place in the chamber. Like the Senate Chamber, the House Chamber has a gallery on the second floor for visitors and journalists.

Senate Chamber The Senate Chamber is a rectangular, two-story room in the center of the north wing. There is a visitor's gallery above it on four sides of the room. The chamber features 100 desks arranged in a semicircle. This is where the nation's 100 senators sit. The seats face a platform at the front of the room. The current vice-president and the Senate's office staff sit on this platform. The vice-president serves as the president of the Senate.

Traditionally, the Republicans sit on the left side of the Senate Chamber. The Democrats sit on the right.

Hall of Columns The Hall of Columns is a dramatic, high-ceilinged corridor that is more than 100 feet (30 m) long. Lining the hall are 28 white marble Corinthian columns. The hall contains a collection of bronze and marble sculptures. The sculptures were donated to the Capitol by each state to honor its notable citizens.

The Hall of Columns is located directly underneath the hall leading into the House of Representatives.

Big Ideas behind the Capitol

The Capitol was built to represent the United States legislature to its citizens and to the world. It had to be an impressive building. The building's designers needed to create a structure that expressed the grandeur and importance of the U.S. government.

The dome is shorter and wider than originally planned. Its shape had to be adjusted to handle the weight of the Statue of Freedom.

Dome Building

The Capitol's dome is its most identifiable feature. Creating a dome of this size took careful planning. It had to be strong and stable. Domes are considered one of the strongest structures that can be built. A dome curves both horizontally and vertically. This double curve evenly distributes the weight of the dome throughout the structure. The weight of the top spreads down in such a way that no one area receives more pressure than the other. The dome is able to bear its own weight and deal with environmental stresses, such as wind and snow, because of its design.

Sandstone

The Capitol's builders chose sandstone as its main building material. It was used to construct the exterior of the Capitol as well as the interior floors and walls. Sandstone was used because it was available in a government-owned **quarry**. It was also easy to cut and shape. However, sandstone is a soft rock. When exposed to weather, such as rain, ice, and snow, over a long period of time, it can begin to crumble and crack. When this happened to the exterior of the Capitol, the sandstone was covered over or replaced with either marble or limestone. These two types of rock are better able to withstand the effects of **weathering**.

The original sandstone can still be seen on the floors and walls inside the building, where weather has little impact.

Science at Work in the Capitol

Building the Capitol required planning, materials, machinery, and physical labor. Power tools did not exist at the time of construction, so the designers had to use simple machines to help ease the workload. Simple machines use scientific principles to make a hard job easier.

Chisels and mallets are often used together. The mallet is struck against the end of the chisel to apply the force needed to push objects apart.

Chisels

Chisels are tools used to cut wood and stone. They were used during the construction of the Capitol. Quarry workers used them to break pieces of rock. Sculptors used them to carve the columns and statues found throughout the building. A chisel is a type of simple machine called a wedge. It is wider at one end than the other. When edged between two objects, a wedge pushes the two objects apart. It does this by converting force on one end into a splitting motion at the other end. The splitting occurs at right angles to the pointed part of the wedge.

Pulleys

During the construction of the Capitol, derricks were used to lift materials into place. A derrick is similar to a crane. It uses a simple machine called a pulley to make lifting easier. A pulley consists of a wheel with a grooved rim through which a cable or chain is guided. Pulleys help raise and lower heavy objects by changing the direction of the pulling force. Pulling on one side of the cable causes the wheel to turn. This moves the other end of the cable in the opposite direction, lifting the object that is connected to that end.

A derrick was used to lift the ironwork of the Capitol's dome into place.

VIRTUAL TOUR

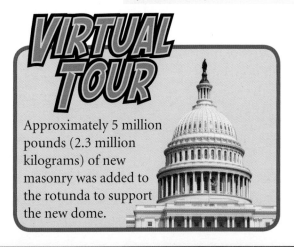

Approximately 5 million pounds (2.3 million kilograms) of new masonry was added to the rotunda to support the new dome.

The Capitol Builders

The United States Capitol has had many builders over the years. Each made a unique contribution to the structure through architecture, engineering, design, sculpting, or other artistries.

In 1802, Thornton was put in charge of the U.S. Patent Office, where he supervised the registrations of inventions and trademarks.

Dr. William Thornton Designer

Dr. William Thornton designed the original concept for the Capitol. Born in the British West Indies in 1759, he later attended school in Scotland, where he graduated as a medical doctor. He moved to the United States in the 1780s, settling in Washington in 1794. Thornton had a wide range of interests, including architecture. When the contest to design the Capitol opened, he decided to submit his ideas. He received $500 and a building lot when his design won the contest.

Stephen Hallet Architect

Stephen Hallet received his architect training in France, graduating in 1785. He arrived in the United States five years later and began working for Pierre Charles L'Enfant, Washington's city planner. Like Thornton, Hallet entered the Capitol's design contest. His entry placed second. However, due to his experience, Hallet was asked to supervise the actual construction of the building. He began making unauthorized design changes and was dismissed from the project in 1794. He was replaced by George Hadfield, who was also dismissed for similar reasons.

Hallet's Capitol design shared certain features with Thornton's plan. Both designs included symmetrical features and a dome.

James Hoban Architect

James Hoban studied architecture at the Dublin Society School. He emigrated from Ireland to Philadelphia in 1785 and later moved to South Carolina. In 1792, Hoban won the design competition for the President's House, known today as the White House, and was put in charge of its construction. He was also asked to manage the construction of the Capitol and was supervisor to both Hallet and Hadfield. When both were dismissed, he took on the day-to-day job of supervising the building's construction.

Hoban's major contribution to the Capitol was designing the interior of the north wing and supervising its completion.

Quarry Workers

Quarry workers performed hard, manual labor in the construction of the Capitol. First, they had to remove mud, dirt, and debris from the surface of the stones in the quarry. Then, they chipped, cut, broke, and shaped the stones with chisels and mallets. Stone was then carried out of the quarry by hand and on shovels. It was placed on barges and shipped down the Potomac River to the construction site. Many African American slaves were put to work quarrying the rock for the Capitol.

Today, quarry workers have the advantage of power tools. Cutting rock can be done quickly and with more ease as a result.

Sculptors

Sculptors are artists who mold objects from a variety of materials, including marble and bronze. They usually draw a plan for the finished project they hope to create. After completing the rough sketch, they take the materials and begin working on them with a variety of tools, including chisels, knives, and hammers. The Capitol's sculptors were responsible for creating the statues, plaques, and ornate doors found throughout the building.

Creating a work of art, such as a sculpture, requires creativity and attention to detail.

Laborers

Laborers contributed much to the actual construction work on the Capitol. They hauled materials to the construction site and helped place them into position on the building. This involved lifting pieces of stone by hand and operating the derricks for larger pieces. Laborers also built the scaffolding and ramps that allowed the work to proceed as the building grew higher. Today, laborers continue to play a key role in the construction process. They know how to use tools, such as drills and jackhammers, and can operate a variety of other construction equipment.

General laborers are found on most construction sites. Their flexible skills allow them to perform a variety of jobs on the construction site.

Similar Structures around the World

Neoclassical structures like the Capitol are found all over the world. All share the columns, pediments, and symmetry of this design style. Many are protected by governments to preserve them.

Monticello

BUILT: 1769–1784, with additional construction from 1796–1809
LOCATION: Charlottesville, Virginia
DESIGN: Thomas Jefferson
DESCRIPTION: Monticello was the home of Thomas Jefferson, the third president of the United States. Like many neoclassical buildings, the house features a dome, columns, and porticoes. In 1987, Monticello was designated a **UNESCO World Heritage Site**, ensuring its preservation for years to come.

Like most neoclassical buildings, the front of the Pantheon features columns that support a pediment.

Monticello is now a museum. Visitors can tour the cellar and the ground floor. The dome is only accessible through special programs.

Pantheon

BUILT: 1758–1789
LOCATION: Paris, France
DESIGN: Jacques-Germaine Soufflot
DESCRIPTION: Located in the Latin Quarter of Paris, France, the Pantheon was originally built as a church. It now functions mainly as a **mausoleum**. Several important writers and historical figures, including writer Victor Hugo and scientist Marie Curie, are buried there.

Massachusetts State House

BUILT: 1798
LOCATION: Boston, Massachusetts
DESIGN: Charles Bullfinch
DESCRIPTION: The Massachusetts State House is home to the state legislature and also houses the governor's offices. The building's dome was originally made of wood shingles. To stop water from leaking inside, it was later covered with a 23-karat gold coating. The dome is topped by a pine cone to show the importance of the lumber industry to the state.

In 1802, the dome was coated with copper. It was then painted gray and later gold. The 23-karat gold coating was applied for the first time in 1874.

White House

BUILT: 1789–1800, with additional construction in 1902 and 1942
LOCATION: Washington, D.C.
DESIGN: James Hoban
DESCRIPTION: The White House was built to be the official residence of the president of the United States. It is the oldest public building in Washington, D.C. The building consists of three main parts. The central building is where the president lives. The West Wing contains the offices of the president and his staff. The First Lady's offices are found in the East Wing.

Even though George Washington commissioned the construction of the White House, he never lived in it. John Adams, the country's second president, was the first president to live in the White House.

Issues Facing the Capitol

The Capitol was built using some of the most durable materials of the era. However, over the years, even materials of the highest quality can experience damage and wear. This is especially true when they sit exposed and unprotected in a natural environment.

WHAT IS THE ISSUE?	
Acid rain is causing the limestone and marble of the Capitol to **corrode**.	Weathering has created at least 1,300 cracks and breaks in the Capitol dome.

EFFECTS	
Marble and limestone structures are composed of **calcium carbonate**, which dissolves easily in acid. The Capitol's marble columns and their square bases have become pitted.	Water is leaking into the rotunda, causing rusting and staining on the rotunda's decorative features.

ACTION TAKEN	
Scientists are working to learn more about acid rain. They have gathered samples of the building stones and are performing tests to determine the best way to fix the deterioration.	A program to repair and restore the Capitol's dome was approved in 2011. Work began on the lower part of the dome in 2012. Plans are in place to restore the remainder of the dome in the coming years.

How Corrosion Works

Buildings and statues made of marble and limestone are especially vulnerable to acid rain. This is because the rock contains large amounts of calcium carbonate. When acids in rain make contact with the calcium carbonate, the stone begins to corrode. Over time, the pieces of the stone dissolve or flake off, weakening the structure. Try this experiment to see how acidic liquids can affect a structure.

Materials
- 2 pieces of chalk
- 2 bowls
- water
- vinegar

Instructions
1. Fill one bowl with water. Pour vinegar into the other bowl.

2. Place one piece of chalk in each bowl.

3. Note how each piece of chalk reacts to the liquid. The chalk placed in the vinegar should begin to fizz. This is the acid in the vinegar reacting with the calcium carbonate in the chalk.

4. Leave the chalk soaking in the bowls overnight.

5. In the morning, remove the chalk from the bowls. Do they look different? What has happened to each piece of chalk? Which liquid is most like acid rain? Why?

Capitol Quiz

Q What is the name of the statue that sits at the top of the Capitol dome?

A The Statue of Freedom

Q How many marble Corinthian columns are in the Hall of Columns?

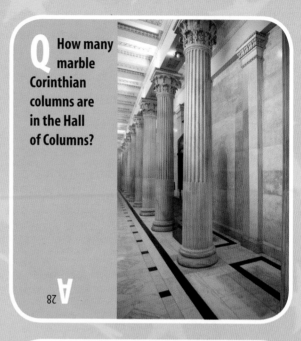

A 28

Q What are the four key features of Neoclassical architecture?

A Tall columns, symmetrical shapes, domed roofs, and pediments

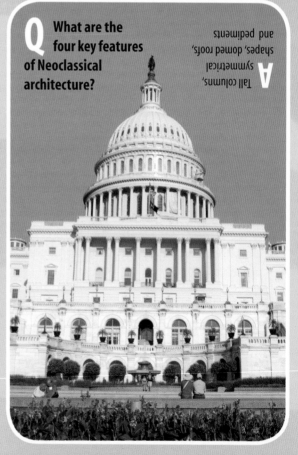

Q When did George Washington lay the cornerstone for the Capitol?

A September 18, 1793

Key Words

acid rain: precipitation containing pollution that can harm the environment

architects: people trained in the planning, design and supervision of the construction of buildings

bicameral: a legislative body that has two houses or chambers

calcium carbonate: a chemical compound found in rocks

cast iron: an alloy of iron and carbon that is put into a mold for shaping

cornerstone: a stone placed at the corner of a building during a ceremony to mark the start of construction

corrode: to wear away an object by a chemical action

engineer: someone who applies scientific principles to the design of structures

focal point: the central point of attention

frieze: a decoration or series of decorations forming an ornamental band around a room

ideals: worthy principles or goals

legislature: an assembly of people who have the power to pass and change laws

mall: a shaded avenue or walkway

mausoleum: a building housing one or more tombs

pediments: triangular gables that appear over porches and often contain sculptures

pilasters: rectangular columns that project from a wall

quadrants: areas that individually make up one quarter of a larger area

quarry: a place where rock is extracted from the ground

restoration: the return of something to its original condition

scrolls: ornamental designs that resemble rolled paper

UNESCO World Heritage Site: a site designated by the United Nations to be of great cultural worth to the world and in need of protection

War of 1812: a war between Great Britain and the United States, fought chiefly along the Canadian border from 1812 to 1814

weathering: the breaking down of rocks and other materials by the action of wind, rain, and other elements

wing: a structure attached to and connected internally with the side of a building

Index

Log on to www.av2books.com

AV² by Weigl brings you media enhanced books that support active learning. Go to www.av2books.com, and enter the special code found on page 2 of this book. You will gain access to enriched and enhanced content that supplements and complements this book. Content includes video, audio, weblinks, quizzes, a slide show, and activities.

AV² Online Navigation

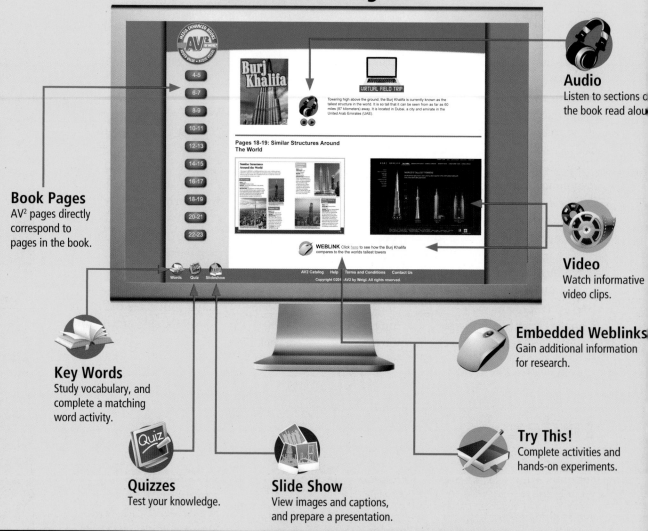

Book Pages
AV² pages directly correspond to pages in the book.

Key Words
Study vocabulary, and complete a matching word activity.

Quizzes
Test your knowledge.

Slide Show
View images and captions, and prepare a presentation.

Audio
Listen to sections of the book read aloud.

Video
Watch informative video clips.

Embedded Weblinks
Gain additional information for research.

Try This!
Complete activities and hands-on experiments.

AV² was built to bridge the gap between print and digital. We encourage you to tell us what you like and what you want to see in the future.

Sign up to be an AV² Ambassador at www.av2books.com/ambassador.